Modern Curriculum Press
BEGINNING
TO
READ
Series

Mabel

Illustrations by Katherine Evans

Library of Congress Catalog Card Number: 58-7296

ISBN 0-8136-5046-1 (Hardbound)
ISBN 0-8136-5546-3 (Paperback)

20 19 18 17 16 15 14 13 12   04 03 02 01 00

the Whale

by Patricia King

Mabel was a whale.

She lived in the Pacific Ocean.

The water was very deep.

The water was very blue.

Mabel was a happy whale.

She lived with her cousins.

She played with her cousins.

They swam in the deep blue ocean.

One day some men came.
They came in a ship.
The men caught Mabel.
They did not hurt her.
They put Mabel in the ship.

Then the men took Mabel away
from the deep blue ocean.

They took her to live in a place
called Marineland.

In Marineland fish and sea animals live in big pools or tanks.

People come to see all the fish and sea animals.

Mabel was put into a tank.

The tank was small.

The water was not deep or blue.

The water was not deep at all.

Mabel could not hide in it.

The sun shone down.

It was very hot.

Mabel could not hide her top fin under the water.

So the hot sun burned Mabel's fin.

11

People came to see Mabel.

They looked at her through the glass.

The people liked Mabel.

But Mabel did not like the tank.
She did not like the water.

The water was not deep.

Mabel could not hide her top fin
under the water.

Mabel was very unhappy,
and she was very sad.

Her fin hurt.

She lay on the bottom of the tank,
but she could not hide her fin.

The sun still burned it.

Soon Mabel was very sick.

The doctor came to see Mabel.
He looked at her from head to tail.
The doctor saw the sunburned fin.
He knew that fin hurt Mabel.
Then the doctor told the men at
Marineland how to help Mabel.

The men put a cool cream on her fin.

The cool cream was for sunburn.

Then the men put an old bag over the fin.

The sun could not burn through the bag.

It could not hurt the fin now.

But Mabel did not feel any better.
She was still a very unhappy whale.
She even stopped eating.

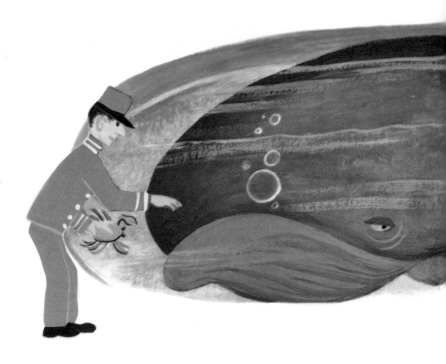

Mabel was very sad.
Everyone wanted to help her.
They thought and thought.
What could they do?

Then the men at Marineland had
an idea.

There was a very big round tank
in Marineland.

If they moved Mabel to the
big tank, she would have more water.

How could they move Mabel?
It would not be easy.
 The men thought and thought.

At last the men brought a big,
big crane.

Then they brought many mattresses.
Then they brought a raft.

They put the mattresses on the
raft.

They put Mabel on the mattresses.

Then the men lifted the raft,
the mattresses, and Mabel
with the big, big crane.

They put the raft, the mattresses, and Mabel on a big truck.

The truck moved Mabel to the big tank.

Then Mabel was lifted fifty feet
up into the air with the crane.
She was put into her new big tank.

Then the doctor gave Mabel
some shots.

They were whale-sized shots.

The shots kept Mabel quiet until
she got used to her new tank.

The shots made Mabel feel better.

Then a man walked Mabel around
and around in her new tank.

He walked her around the tank
so she would get to know it.

Soon Mabel felt better.

She swam around her new tank.

The water was deep.

The water covered Mabel's fin.

The sun did not shine on the fin
and burn it.

Mabel was happy.

Before long, Mabel blew!
It was a happy spray.

Mabel was a happy whale.

Everyone at Marineland was happy
because Mabel was well again.

MABEL THE WHALE

Mabel the Whale has a total vocabulary of 161 words. Regular plurals (-*s*) and regular verb forms (-*s, -ed, -ing*) of words already on the list are not listed separately, but the endings are given in parentheses after the words.

5	Mabel		cousins		took
	was		played		away
	a		they		from
	whale		swam		to
	she		too		place
	live(d)	**7**	one		called
	in		day		Marineland
	the		some	**9**	fish
	Pacific		men		and
	Ocean		came		sea
	water		ship		animals
	very		caught		big
	deep		did		pools
	blue		not		or
6	happy		hurt		tanks
	with		put		people
	her	**8**	then		come

see
all
10 into
small
at
could
hide
it
11 sun
shone
down
hot
top
fin
under
so
burn(ed)
12 looked
through
liked
glass
but
13 unhappy
sad
lay
on
bottom
of
still
soon
sick
14 doctor
he
head
tail
saw
sunburned

knew
that
told
how
help
15 cool
cream
for
an
old
bag
over
now
16 feel
any
better
even
stopped
eating
everyone
wanted
thought
what
do
17 had
idea
there
round
if
move(d)
would
have
more
18 be
easy
19 last
brought

crane
many
mattresses
raft
21 lifted
22 truck
23 fifty
feet
up
air
new
24 gave
shots
were
whale-sized
kept
quiet
until
got
used
25 made
man
walked
around
get
know
26 felt
covered
shine
27 before
long
blew
spray
because
well
again

29